I·N·S·I·D·E

AUSTRALIA

Ian James

Franklin Watts
London · New York · Sydney · Toronto

CONTENTS

The land	4
The people and their history	7
Towns and cities	10
Family life	15
Food	17
Sports and pastimes	19
The arts	21
Farming	23
Industry	25
Looking to the future	28
Facts about Australia	30
Map of Australia	31
Index	32

© 1989 Franklin Watts
96 Leonard Street
London EC2

Published in the USA by
Franklin Watts Inc.
387 Park Avenue South
New York, N.Y. 10016

Franklin Watts Australia
14 Mars Road
Lane Cove
NSW 2066

Design: K & Co
Illustrations: Hayward Art Group

UK ISBN: 0 86313 836 5
US ISBN: 0-531-10759-0
Library of Congress Catalog
Card Number: 89-5840

Phototypeset by Lineage Ltd, Watford
Printed in Belgium

Front cover: ZEFA
Back cover: Chris Fairclough
Frontispiece: Hutchison Library

Photographs: Australia House 4, 7,
8, 10, 13, 21; Chris Fairclough 5t, 6,
11, 12, 15, 16t, 16b, 17, 18t, 18b, 19,
20, 24t, 24b, 25, 27, 28, 29, 30; Hulton
Picture Library 9t; Hutchison
Library 5b; NSW Dept. of
Education 23; S.A. Dept. of Tourism
14; the Tate Gallery, London 22;
ZEFA 9b.

The land

Although it is surrounded by water, Australia is regarded not as an island, but as a continent. It is the only country that is also a continent. Its official name is the Commonwealth of Australia.

Australia is in the southern hemisphere. It faces the Indian Ocean in the west and south, and the Pacific Ocean in the north and east. The best known feature of its coastline is the world's largest coral formation, the Great Barrier Reef.

Australia is the flattest continent. Only 5 per cent of the country is more than 600 m (about 1,970 ft) above sea level. The three main land regions are the Western Plateau, the Central Lowlands, and the Eastern Highlands.

Below: **The Great Barrier Reef, consisting of coral reefs and islands, extends about 2,000 km (1,240 miles) off Australia's northeast coast.**

Above: **The Eastern Highlands, or the Great Dividing Range, include the scenic Blue Mountains near Sydney.**

Left: **Australia's longest permanently flowing river, the Murray, rises in the Eastern Highlands and flows across the Central Lowlands. Its tributary, the Darling, is longer, but it dries up in summer.**

5

The Western Plateau covers two-thirds of Australia. It is mostly flat, although there are some low mountains, including Ayers Rock in Northern Territory. The Central Lowlands run north-south between the Western Plateau and the Eastern Highlands, which are also called the Great Dividing Range. This range includes Australia's highest peak, Mount Kosciusko.

The Western Plateau is hot and dry, with some vast deserts. The Central Lowlands are dry grassland, but ranchers get water from wells sunk into the ground. The tropical north, the Eastern Highlands and the eastern and southeastern coasts have ample rainfall but lots of sunshine too.

Above: **The Olgas, in Northern Territory, near Ayers Rock, are low peaks that rise above the generally flat Western Plateau.**

6

The people and their history

The first, or Aboriginal, people of Australia arrived from Asia more than 40,000 years ago. They lived in harmony with nature, hunting and gathering their food, knowing where to find water. Their religion embraces myths about the creation of the world and the idea that the spirits of their ancestors inhabit every part of the land.

When Europeans first settled in Australia in 1788, the Aboriginal people numbered about 300,000. They were divided into about 50 main language groups. But their numbers were reduced as they clashed with Europeans, and died of European diseases to which they had no resistance. In 1930, there were only about 70,000 Aboriginal people left. Today, there are 230,000.

Below: **The Aboriginal people of Australia often use religious subjects in their paintings.**

Dutch sailors explored parts of Australia's north and west coasts in the 17th century. They thought the dry land was valueless. But in 1770, Captain James Cook explored the pleasant eastern shores and made them a British possession. The first British settlements were colonies for convicts, but soon free settlers began to set up farms and search for minerals. Gold was discovered in the 1850s.

Australia became independent on January 1, 1901, when Britain's six Australian colonies became states and united together. Until World War II, most Australians were descended from people from the British Isles. Since 1945, many immigrants have come from mainland Europe, and more recently, from Asia.

Below: **Captain James Cook explored the east coast of Australia in 1770. He named it New South Wales.**

Above: **Australian soldiers fought bravely at Gallipoli in Turkey in 1915 and 1916. Australia also fought alongside Britain in World War II.**

Left: **Canberra, in the Australian Capital Territory, has been the national capital since 1927.**

Towns and Cities

Today, 86 per cent of Australians live in cities or towns. More than 60 per cent of the people live in the state capitals. In order of size, these are Sydney (capital of New South Wales), Melbourne (Victoria), Brisbane (Queensland), Perth (Western Australia), Adelaide (South Australia), Canberra (Australian Capital Territory), Hobart (Tasmania) and Darwin (Northern Territory).

The people in rural areas around the towns, which Australians call the bush, live in small farm settlements. Others live in the outback the remote interior, in farm and road houses. The Flying Doctor Service, which began in 1928, and the School of the Air which began in 1950, provide health and educational services in the outback.

Below: **Children in remote areas get their primary and secondary education through the School of the Air. They use two-way radios to talk with their teachers.**

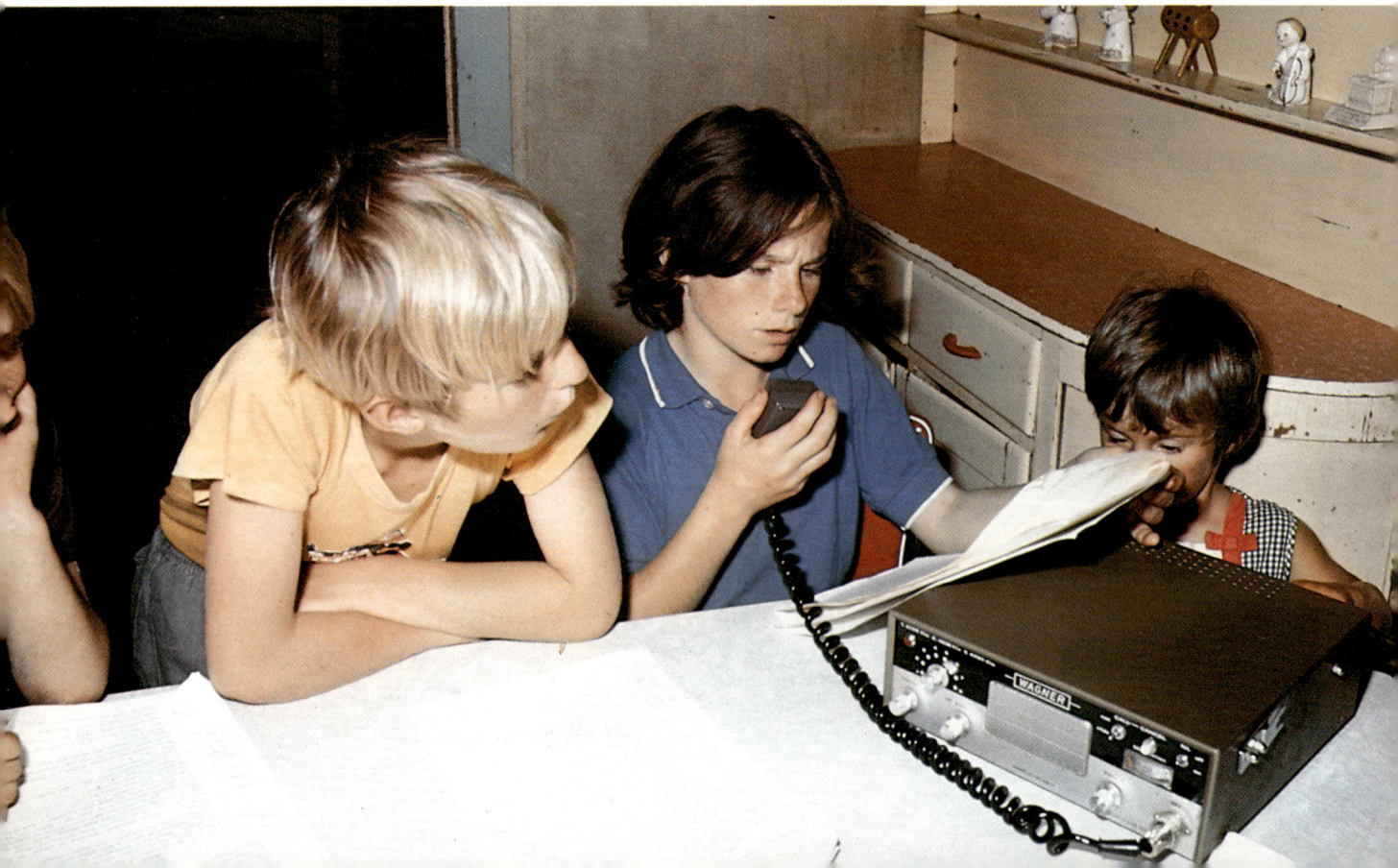

Above: **Sydney's skyline includes modern skyscrapers and the shell-like Opera House.**

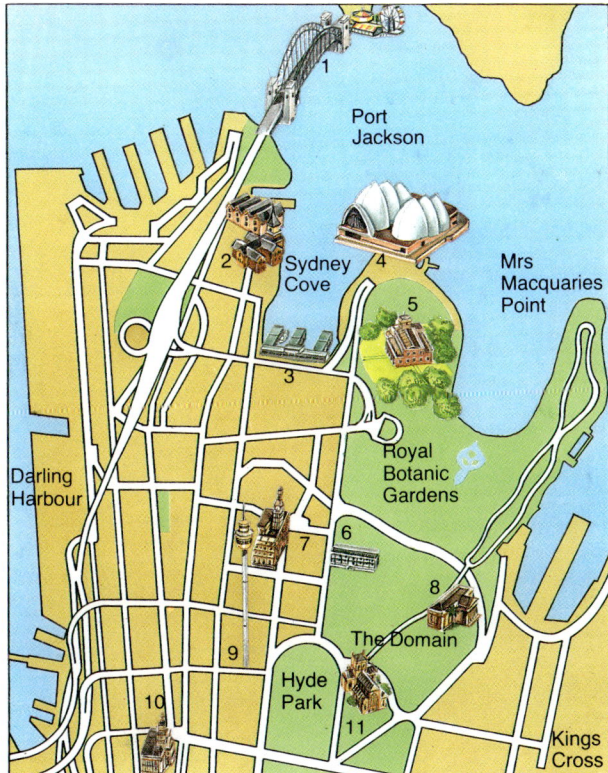

Left: **The map shows some of Sydney's landmarks.**

1 Harbour Bridge
2 The Rocks Visitors Centre
3 Circular Quay
4 Opera House
5 Government House
6 Parliament House
7 Martin Place
8 Art Gallery
9 Sydney Tower
10 Town Hall
11 St Mary's Cathedral

Most Australians live in cities on the moist but sunny coastlands, especially in the east and southeast. The largest city, Sydney, has one of the world's finest ports. It is a bustling, prosperous city which includes the site of the first British settlement, set up in 1788. Its superb beaches, such as Bondi beach, attract many tourists, but it is also Australia's leading industrial city.

Melbourne, the second largest city, has broad, straight streets and large areas of parkland. It was founded in 1835 and grew during the Gold Rush in the 1850s. It is a major financial, industrial and cultural city.

Below: **Melbourne has an electric tramway system for journeys up to 10 km (6 miles).**

Map labels:
Darwin
Port Hedland
Dampier
Gladstone
Brisbane
Gold Coast
Perth
Fremantle
Whyalla
Adelaide
Newcastle
Sydney
Melbourne
Wollongong
Canberra
Geelong
Western Port
Hobart

Legend:
🏢 Major cities
— Main routeways
🚢 Main ports

Above: **The map shows major routes and cities in Australia.**

Left: **Darwin, capital of Northern Territory, is a small but modern city.**

Brisbane was founded in 1824 as a colony for convicts. Adelaide, in the south, was first settled in 1836. The world's most isolated city is Perth in West Australia. Adelaide, the nearest state capital, is farther away from Perth than London is from Moscow, or New York City from Denver.

Canberra, the country's capital since 1927, was beautifully planned by an American architect, Walter Burley Griffin. Hobart, which was founded in 1804 as a port, has many early 19th-century buildings. By contrast Darwin, the small capital of Northern Territory, has been almost entirely rebuilt since it was flattened by a cyclone on Christmas Day 1974.

Above: **Rundle Mall, which is reserved for people on foot, is Adelaide's busiest shopping street.**

Family life

Most Australians have a high standard of living. More than 70 per cent own their own homes. Most families live in detached, brick houses, with large gardens, though an increasing number of people in the inner cities live in apartments. Practically every home has a refrigerator, more than 90 per cent have a washing machine, and 86 per cent have a car. About one tenth of homes in city residential areas has a swimming pool.

Many people go to and leave work early to join their children, who finish school in the mid-afternoon. In summer, many families then go to the beach and often picnic there. About three out of every four families live within 80 km (50 miles) of the sea.

Below: **This isolated farm is in the interior of New South Wales.**

Left: **City houses on the waterfront, like these in Sydney, are popular and expensive to buy.**

Below: **Television viewing is a popular family activity.**

Food

Breakfast usually consists of cereal, toast and tea, the chief hot drink, or coffee. Lunch is often sandwiches. The main meal is in the evening when the family is together. Beer or wine are often drunk with this meal.

Grilled, roasted or barbecued meat, especially beef and lamb, served with potatoes and another vegetable is the leading dish. Seafood, salads and fresh fruit are also very popular.

In recent years, the plain British style of cooking has been challenged. Australians, one third of whom eat out at least once a week, have a wide choice. The cities now have numerous American, Chinese, French, Indian, Indonesian, Italian, Lebanese, Mexican, Vietnamese and other restaurants.

Below: **Many people visit a supermarket once a week to do the bulk of their shopping.**

Above: **Cereals are common breakfast foods.**

Left: **Grilled chops and steaks are often cooked in the kitchen and served to the rest of the family and friends in the garden.**

Sports and pastimes

Because of Australia's wonderful climate, outdoor activities are extremely popular, especially at weekends, and on public and annual holidays, which are often four to five weeks long. Many people enjoy camping or caravanning in the bush, near rivers or lakes, or a family picnic on a beach, where they can scuba-dive, swim, water-ski, or go boating, sailing, and wind-surfing. In recent years, an increasing number of people have taken up the winter sports, such as skiing, in new resorts, especially in the snowy Australian Alps.

Despite the many outdoor activities, most Australians are keen television watchers. Seven out of ten people watch television regularly and three out of ten watch almost every night.

Below: **Most Australians live near the sea, and many young people are good swimmers and surfers.**

Australians of all ages enjoy team games as players or spectators and most major events get extensive television coverage. Cricket is the chief summer game and Australia plays regularly against teams from England, India, New Zealand, Pakistan, Sri Lanka, and the West Indies. Also popular are four forms of football: Australian rules football, Rugby union, Rugby league, and soccer. Horse racing is also followed, and many Australians enjoy gambling.

Australia's sportsmen and women have won international fame. They are especially good at boxing, cycling, golf, motor racing, squash, swimming, tennis, track events, rowing and yachting.

Above: **Large crowds watch international cricket matches. The picture shows Australia playing England in Sydney.**

The arts

The artistic traditions of the Aboriginal Australians are closely linked to their beliefs about the creation of the world and their mythical ancestors. Paintings on bark, stone and cave walls depict mythical heroes who lived in a time long ago called "Dreamtime". The Aborginal people believe that they return to Dreamtime when they sleep. Aborigine arts also include carving, singing, chanting, and spoken literature.

Other arts were developed by European immigrants. A national literature grew up around the start of the 20th century with the bush ballads of A.B. "Banjo" Paterson and the stories of Henry Lawson. The best known writer today is Patrick White, who won the Nobel Prize for literature in 1973.

Below: **Aboriginal artists often paint on bark. Many paintings are concerned with their traditional religious beliefs.**

The Heidelberg school of the 1880s was famous for its Australian landscape painters such as Tom Roberts and Frederick McCubbin. Later on, Sidney Nolan became famous for his paintings depicting Australian folklore. Australia has some beautiful 19th-century architecture. The best known modern building is the Sydney Opera House.

Australia has produced several great performers, including the singers Nellie Melba and Joan Sutherland, and composers, such as Percy Grainger and Malcolm Williamson. In recent years, several film directors, including Gillian Armstrong, Bruce Beresford and Peter Weir, have received international acclaim.

Below: **Sidney Nolan is Australia's best known painter. In the 1940s, he painted a series of works about a famous outlaw named Ned Kelly.**

Farming

Farmland covers about two-thirds of Australia, but most of it is dry grazing land. Only about 7 per cent of Australia is used for growing crops. Farming employs 7 per cent of Australian workers, but they produce nearly all the food the people need.

The interior of Australia contains huge cattle and sheep stations, the Australian term for ranches, and the country is the leading producer and exporter of wool. Australia also exports dairy products, meat and wheat. Sugar cane and tropical fruits grow on the hot east coastlands of Queensland. New South Wales and South Australia produce oranges and South Australia grows grapes for wine-making.

Below: **Wool is a major product in New South Wales and Western Australia. Competitions are sometimes held to find the fastest sheep shearer.**

Above: **Cattle ranches cover large areas of the dry interior of New South Wales.**

Left: **South Australia has large vineyards that grow grapes for making wine.**

Industry

In the last 30 years, Australia has become one of the world's leading exporters of minerals. In 1960, minerals made up 7 per cent of Australia's exports. Today, they account for 40 per cent. Minerals and farm products form more than two thirds of Australia's exports.

Minerals are produced in all parts of the country, but the greatest discoveries in the last 30 years have been in Western Australia. The country leads the world in producing bauxite and lead and is the third largest producer of iron ore, nickel and zinc. It is also one of the top ten producers of coal, copper, gold, manganese, silver, tin, tungsten and uranium. Australia also produces about 70 per cent of its oil needs.

Below: **Huge mines produce a variety of minerals in Western Australia.**

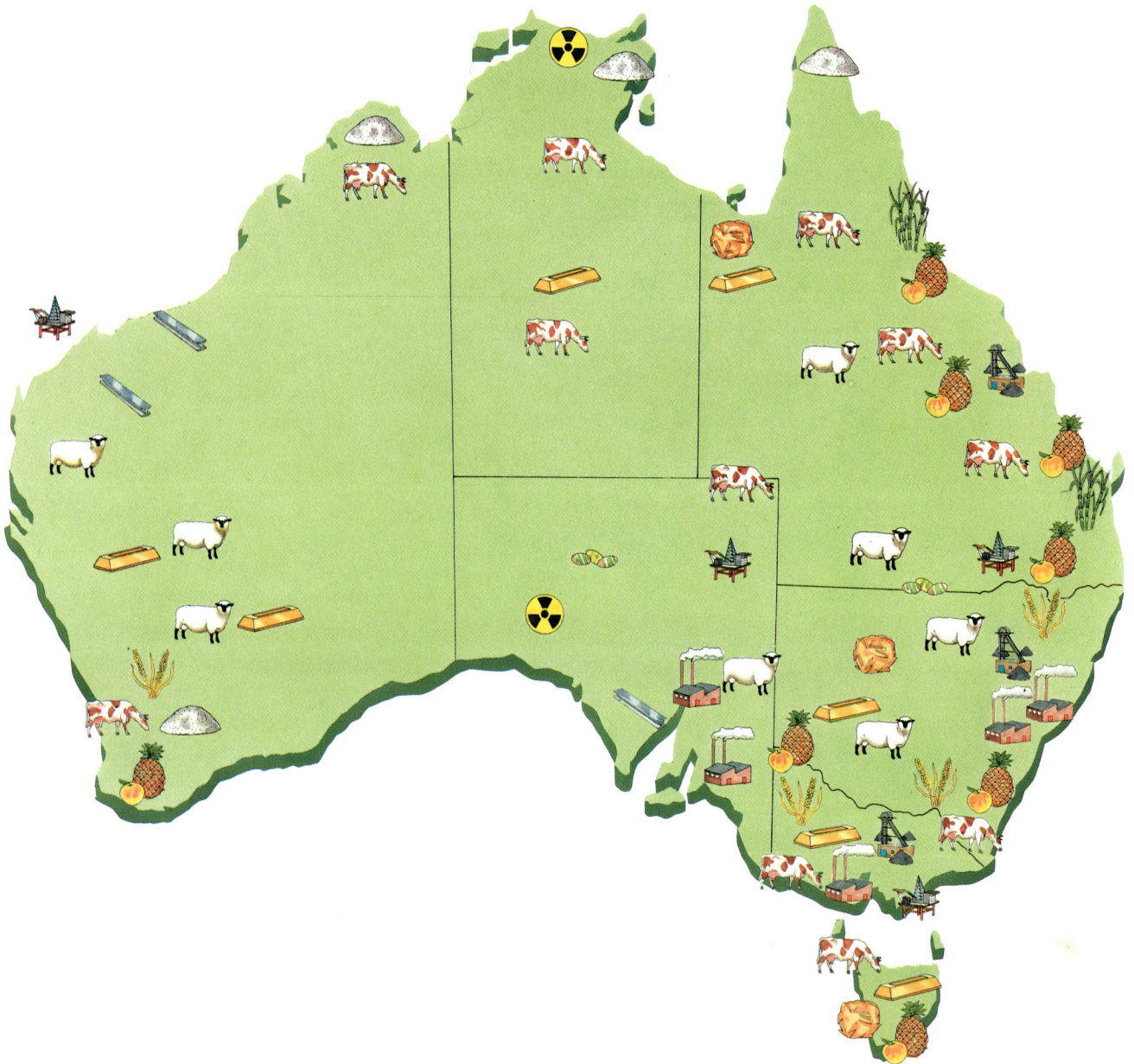

	Iron ore		Uranium
	Bauxite		Industry
	Coal		Wheat
	Oil and gas		Sugar cane
	Copper		Fruit
	Gold and silver		Sheep
	Opals		Cattle

Above: **The map shows some of the economic activities in Australia.**

As well as coal and oil, Australia also uses hydroelectric power. The largest hydroelectric and irrigation project is the Snowy Mountain Scheme in southeast Australia.

Industry employs 32 per cent of Australian workers, while 61 per cent work in services. Most of the goods manufactured in Australia are for its own use. They include processed foods and consumer goods used in the home. Food processing forms the largest part of the country's manufacturing sector. Australia also produces a wide range of producer goods, including factory machines and construction equipment. Other major industries include car assembly, chemical and textile production. The computer industry has grown quickly in recent years.

Below: **Car assembly is an important industry in Victoria.**

Looking to the future

Australia belongs to the Commonwealth of Nations and Britain's Queen is also Queen of Australia, but ties with Britain have loosened recently. Before 1945, most immigrants came from the British Isles. Since then, only one third have been British or Irish. The new immigrants are from other parts of Europe or Asia.

Britain once dominated Australia's trade. This changed in 1973 when Britain joined the European Economic Community. By the mid-1980s, Japan and the United States supplied 55 per cent of Australia's imports and took 38 per cent of its exports. Britain supplied 7 per cent of the imports and took 3 per cent of the exports.

Below: **Aboriginal children will benefit from their parents' successful campaigns for land rights in the 1970s and 1980s.**

Today many Australians see themselves as part of a Pacific Ocean community. Their natural allies are the countries of eastern Asia and the Americas, rather than Britain. Australian troops fought in Vietnam alongside the American forces.

At home, Australia faces several problems. Its economy depends on exporting farm products and minerals. But when world demand for these items falls, Australia is plunged into economic crisis, with rising inflation and unemployment. In future, Australia will also have to compete with the rising industrial nations of Asia. However, most Australians believe that they can overcome their problems and preserve their easy-going way of life.

Above: **Australians from all the ethnic and language groups look forward to the future with optimism.**

Facts about Australia

Area:
7,682,000 sq km
(2,996,200 sq miles)

Population:
16,188,000 (1987)

Capital:
Canberra

Largest cities:
Sydney (pop 3,430,000)
Melbourne (2,942,000)
Brisbane (1,171,000)
Perth (1,025,000)
Adelaide (993,000)
Newcastle (429,000)
Canberra (286,000)
Wollongong (238,000)

Official language:
English

Religion:
Christianity
   (76 per cent)

Main exports:
Metal ores and metal
scrap, coal, cereals,
textiles, including wool,
oil and oil products,
iron and steel,
meat, sugar.

Unit of currency:
Australian dollar

Australia compared with other countries

Australia 2 per sq.km.

Britain 231 per sq.km.

USA 26 per sq.km.

France 100 per sq.km.

Above: **Australia is thinly populated.**

Below: **Australia is smaller than the United States.**

USA

Australia

France   UK

Below: **Some Australian stamps and money.**

Pacific Ocean

BORNEO

SULAWESI

IRIAN JAYA

PAPUA NEW GUINEA

INDONESIA

TIMOR

Arafura Sea

Timor Sea

Darwin

Weipa

Coral Sea

R. Roper

Gulf of Carpentaria

Great Barrier Reef

Indian Ocean

Wyndham

R. Victoria

NORTHERN TERRITORY

R. Mitchell

Cooktown

R. Gilbert

Cairns

Kimberley Plateau

Derby

Tennant Creek

Cloncurry

R. Flinders

Townsville

Bowen

Broome

R. Fitzroy

Mackay

R. Georgina

R. Belyando

Great Sandy Desert

QUEENSLAND

Port Hedland

Dampier

Macdonnell Ranges

Alice Springs

R. Thomson

Rockhampton

Hamersley Range

R. Ashburton

Tropic of Capricorn

Bundaberg

Ayers Rock

R. Finke

R. Diamantina

Mt Newman

Gibson Desert

Musgrave Ranges

Charleville

Great Dividing

R. Gascoyne

R. Murchison

Carnarvon

WESTERN AUSTRALIA

Oodnadatta

Toowoomba

Brisbane

Lake Eyre

Warwick

Gold Coast

SOUTH AUSTRALIA

Lismore

Lake Barlee

Great Victoria Desert

Lake Torrens

Woomera

Flinders Range

R. Darling

NEW SOUTH WALES

Tamworth

Port Macquarie

Geraldton

Kalgoorlie

Lake Gairdner

Broken Hill

Dubbo

Maitland

Nullarbor Plain

Port Augusta

Range

Whyalla

R. Lachlan

Newcastle

Perth

Port Pirie

R. Murray

Wagga Wagga

Sydney

Fremantle

Narrogin

Esperance

Adelaide

R. Murray

Albury

Wollongong

Bunbury

Great Australian Bight

Canberra (ACT)

Albany

VICTORIA

Mt Kosciusko

Bendigo

Australian Alps

Ballarat

Warrnambool

Melbourne

Geelong

Southern Ocean

Bass Strait

Tasman Sea

Devonport

Launceston

Queenstown

TASMANIA

Hobart

Index

Aboriginal Australians 7, 21, 28
Adelaide 10, 14
Architecture 22
Australian Capital Territory 9-10
Armstrong, Gillian 22
Australian rules football 20
Ayers Rock 6

Beresford, Bruce 22
Blue Mountains 5
Bondi beach 12
Brisbane 10, 14
Bush 10

Camping 19
Canberra 9-10, 14
Caravanning 19
Car assembly 27
Cattle 23-24
Central Lowlands 5-6
Climate 6
Commonwealth of Nations 20
Cook, Captain James 8
Cooking 17
Cricket 20
Crops 23

Darling River 5
Darwin 10, 12, 14
"Dreamtime" 21

Eastern Highlands 5-6
Education 10
Exploration 8

Farming 23-24
Flying Doctor Service 10
Fruits 23

Gallipoli 9
Grainger, Percy 22
Great Barrier Reef 4
Great Dividing Range 5-6
Griffin, Walter Burley 14

Heidelberg School 22
History 7-9
Hobart 10
Homes 15
Horse racing 20

Immigration 8, 28
Independence 8
Industry 27

Japan 28

Lawson, Henry 21
Literature 21
Livestock 23-24

Manufacturing 27
McCubbin, Frederick 22
Meals 17-18
Melba, Nellie 22
Melbourne 10, 12
Minerals 25
Murray River 5

New South Wales 8, 10, 15, 23-24
Nolan, Sidney 22
Northern Territory 6, 10, 13-14

Oil 25
Olgas (mountains) 6
Outback 10

Painting 21-22
Paterson, A.B. "Banjo" 21
Perth 10, 14

Queensland 10, 23

Religion, Aboriginal 7, 21
Roberts, Tom 22
Rugby 20

School of the Air 10
Sheep 23
Shopping 17
Snowy Mountains Scheme 27
Soccer 20
South Australia 10, 23-24
Surfing 19
Sutherland, Joan 22
Sydney 10-12, 16, 22

Tasmania 10, 24
Television 16, 19
Trade 28

United States 28

Victoria 10
Vietnam War 29

Water sports 19
Weir, Peter 22
Western Australia 10, 25
Western Plateau 6
White, Patrick 21
Williamson, Malcolm 22
Wine 24
Winter sports 19
Wool 23